GIVING
IS
LIVING

GIVING

IS

LIVING

101 WAYS TO PRACTICE
EFFORTLESS GENEROSITY

MARNIE & TISHA HOWARD

hatherleigh

Hatherleigh Press is committed to preserving and protecting
the natural resources of the Earth. Environmentally responsible
and sustainable practices are embraced within the company's
mission statement.

Hatherleigh Press is a member of the Publishers Earth Alliance,
committed to preserving and protecting the natural resources of the
planet while developing a sustainable business model for the book
publishing industry.

PEA Member   Recycled Content   Earth-Friendly Printing   Cause Supporting

Recycled Content: The interior of this
book is printed on 100% recycled paper.

Earth-Friendly Printing: The interior
of this book was printed with soy ink.

Cause Supporting

hatherleigh

5-22 46th Avenue, Suite 200
Long Island City, NY 11101
www.hatherleighpress.com

Library of Congress Cataloging-in-Publication Data
Howard, Marnie.
Giving is living : 101 ways to practice effortless generosity / Marnie
& Tisha Howard.
p. cm.
ISBN 978-1-57826-290-8 (alk. paper)
1. Social service. 2. Charities. 3. Charity organization. I. Howard,
Tisha. II. Title.
HV40.H682 2008
177'.7–dc22

2008040085

Giving is Living is available for bulk purchase, special promotions,
and premiums. For information on reselling and special purchase
opportunities, call 1-800-528-2550 and ask for
the Special Sales Manager.

10 9 8 7 6 5 4 3
Printed in the United States

Generosity: *noun*

1 a: the quality or fact of being generous

  b: a generous act

2: ABUNDANCE <great *generosity* of spirit>

A NOTE FROM THE PUBLISHER

Ralph Waldo Emerson wrote, "the only gift is a portion of thyself." I believe he meant that all true generosity comes from within, and that the most meaningful gifts are true expressions of who we are and what we value.

Giving is Living is one such gift. Sisters Marnie and Tisha Howard have thoughtfully compiled a list of 101 ways for all of us to practice meaningful giving in our daily lives, and, together, to foster generosity that brightens our world.

As this book will show you, true generosity can be practiced every moment of the day, towards anyone we encounter. Marnie and Tisha share ways we can connect and give to our communities as well as to our immediate families; to strangers as well as to old, dear friends.

To give effortlessly and love unconditionally: these are the building blocks of our better selves and a better world. When we give of ourselves, through politeness or kindness or by volunteering or sharing, we honor our common humanity and improve our common experience.

—ANDREW FLACH, PUBLISHER

A NOTE FROM THE AUTHORS

"One of the best things about being an adult is the realization that you can share with your sister and still have plenty for yourself."
—BETSY COHEN

As sisters, Marnie and Tisha continue to uncover life's lessons together. Those of you with siblings will relate and those of you without siblings can substitute your best friend and you will quickly get the picture. We are two All-American girls who grew up in a small suburban town in Colorado, learning how to love, laugh, cry, and share with one another. In fact, Tisha once stated that her soul's purpose was to come into this world to teach Marnie how to share. As children, we needed guidance to find our way and put order to the world around us. Many lessons were learned, but most important of all was the act of generosity. Learning to give of yourself and to share all of the blessings you have received in this lifetime can create a positive impact on the world and is the ultimate act of kindness and selflessness. You learn that bringing a smile to someone's face helps illuminate your inner smile. Our goal is to make the world a brighter place. We want to remind you how easy it is to enrich the lives of those around you with effortless ways of generosity. Every act of generosity moves us all to a higher purpose. We are all finding our way down life's path, despite color, race, age, religion, sex, or any other wall of difference our society has attempted to create. These differences are simply an illusion. Join us as we journey together, one generous act at a time, to help celebrate the world as ONE.

Safe travels,
Marnie & Tisha

"Be the change you wish
to see in the world."

—Gandhi

GIVING
IS
LIVING

1

Always take a moment to sincerely say, "thank you." It takes almost no time, but makes a huge difference.

2

Smile at a stranger. They just might share the smile with someone in return.

"Let no one ever come to you without leaving better and happier. Be the living expression of God's kindness: kindness in your face, kindness in your eyes, kindness in your smile."

— MOTHER TERESA

3

Honor others with a generous spirit. Start a savings account in memory of someone special to you and donate those funds in their name.

4

Brighten someone's day. Pay the toll, subway, or bus fare for the person behind you.

5

Lend a hand. Hold the door open for someone else, especially if that person's hands are full.

6

Give someone the gift of a
better future. Be a mentor to
an underprivileged child in
your community. Go to mentor.
com for more information.

7

At the store, let someone
go ahead of you in line.
Selflessness can be inspiring
to others.

"Never lose a chance of saying a kind word."

— WILLIAM THACKERAY

8

If you spot someone who looks lost, stop and ask him or her if they need help or directions. A little help can go a long way.

9

Call, write, or e-mail a long
lost friend or a distant relative.
It's never too late to reconnect.

10

Learn the name of the employees at a store you visit regularly, and greet them by name the next time you see them. A personal greeting is meaningful.

11

Share a "small town feeling." Say hello to people you pass on the street.

12

Send a card to your parents
or a friend just to say, "I
appreciate you." It takes just
a little time to show gratitude
for the amazing people in
your life.

"What you do speaks so loudly that I cannot hear what you say."

— RALPH WALDO EMERSON

13

If you spot someone caught in a downpour, offer your umbrella. It'll bring some sunshine to their rainy day.

14

Share the spirit of giving.
Invite a friend to join you on
a volunteer day for a cause
in your community. Go to
charity-charities.org to find
local organizations.

15

Always take an extra moment
to ask someone, "how are you
today?" Showing you care can
be the greatest gift of all.

16

Invite a new group member, neighbor, or co-worker out to lunch. A warm welcome is never forgotten.

17

Leave a favorite book at a local café for someone to enjoy. Or check out bookcrossing.com for more ideas on how to share your books with others. Knowledge is a powerful gift.

"We make a living by what we get, but we make a life by what we give"

— WINSTON CHURCHILL

18

If you spot someone in the store who can't get an item on a high shelf, offer to reach for it or find help from a store employee. Generosity can make you feel larger than life!

19

Ask if you can help. The next time you are going to the store, offer to pick something up for a neighbor.

20

Donate anything you no longer need or wear to charity. Your old clothes can do good for someone in need—and it won't cost you a penny.

21

The next time you get together
with a friend, greet him or
her with a hug. It only takes
a moment, but the warmth of
your gesture will last all day.

5 GENEROUS ACTS
THAT TAKE NO TIME

HOLD THE DOOR OPEN FOR A
   STRANGER.
LET SOMEONE GO AHEAD OF YOU
   IN LINE AT THE MARKET.
CALL A LONG-LOST FRIEND TO SAY
   HELLO.
LEAVE A LITTLE CHANGE IN THE
   TIP JAR.
GIVE TO CHARITY WHEN
   YOU SEARCH THE WEB AT
   GOODSEARCH.COM.

22

Celebrate someone special to you. Make a list of all of your friends' birthdays, and call them on their big day!

23

Strengthen family ties. At the next family get together, take the time to speak to an older relative.

"*Complete possession is proved
only by giving. All you are
unable to give possesses you.*"

— ANDRE GIDE

24

Make a day easier for someone.
Offer to give a friend, neighbor,
or co-worker a ride if his or her
car is in the shop.

25

Introduce two of your friends
who have never met. The more,
the merrier!

26

Learn the name of your postal carrier and greet him or her the next time you see each other. Showing appreciation for others is free!

27

Spread good will at work.
Bring bagels to share with
your co-workers.

5 GENEROUS PHRASES

"PLEASE."

"THANK YOU."

"YOU ARE WELCOME."

"PARDON ME."

"AFTER YOU."

28

Give a treat! Bring something yummy for the staff at your next doctor's appointment.

29

Set up recycling bins at home
or around the office and then
visit earth911.org for tons of
green tips. Consider this
generosity towards the earth.

"The happiness of life is made up of minute fractions—the little soon-forgotten charities of a kiss, a smile, a kind look, a heartfelt compliment in the disguise of a playful raillery, and the countless other infinitessimals of pleasurable thought and genial feeling."

— SAMUEL TAYLOR COLERIDGE

30

Inspire. Share a book that is special to you with a friend, co-worker, or acquaintance.

31

Give without being asked. In home or at the office, put a fresh pot of coffee on—even if you don't want any yourself.

32

Give blood or volunteer to help out at the blood drive. Go to your local Red Cross office or visit redcross.org for details. Your contribution could save a life.

33

Look for a chance to be generous. If you spot an elderly individual who is struggling with their groceries, offer to help.

34

Reach just a little further.
When you are shoveling snow,
clear some from your
neighbor's sidewalk, too.

35

If you receive excellent service, write a letter to the employee's supervisor to let them know. Your appreciation could lead to career advancement for someone deserving.

36

Donate to a disaster relief fund. Give to others as you hope they would give to you.

"Who is the happiest of men? He who values the merits of others, and in their pleasure takes joy, even as though 'twere his own."

—Johann Wolfgang von Goethe

37

Giving can be simple. Donate old magazines to soldiers overseas. Visit uso.org for more details.

38

The next time you buy
something special for yourself,
donate an amount equal to
the item's cost. Whenever
you enjoy your new purchase,
you will remember your act
of generosity, and the good
feeling will warm your heart.

39

Reunite others. Organize a dinner with a group of neighbors, co-workers, or friends you haven't seen in a while.

*"Try not to become a man of
success but a man of value."*

— ALBERT EINSTEIN

40

Be an active supporter of the arts. Visit a local museum, theater, or gallery.

41

Give your friends or neighbors a break. Babysit their kids for free so they can enjoy a night out.

42

Share your skills. Whether you
can knit, sew, build, or bake,
you can find an organization
on-line that can put your
talents to use for a good cause.

"You're happiest while you're making the greatest contribution."

— ROBERT F. KENNEDY

43

Give for fun! Surprise a loved
one with a homemade meal.

44

Stay in touch. Update your
address book so you don't lose
touch with friends.

45

Be attentive. The next time
a friend has a problem, take
the time to listen carefully
to the dilemma and offer
encouragement and support.

46

Offer to collect unwanted
books from your neighbors or
friends and donate them to the
local library. You will empower
the minds in your community.

5 GENEROUS ACTS TO DO AS A FAMILY

VOLUNTEER FOR A COMMUNITY PROJECT.

WORK TOGETHER TO HOST A FUNDRAISING YARD SALE OR BAKE SALE. DONATE ALL THE PROCEEDS TO A LOCAL CHARITY.

WRITE A LETTER TO A DISTANT RELATIVE.

CREATE AND GIVE A PHOTO ALBUM TO A BELOVED GRANDPARENT.

SHARE HOUSEHOLD CHORES WILLINGLY. GIVE MOM OR DAD A BREAK.

47

Reach out. Print out a map with the addresses for local homeless shelters, and share it with the next person you see who is sleeping on the streets.

48

Make a difference. If there is
a park in your neighborhood
that is run down, organize a
community effort to clean it up.

49

Give kindness. Every day for
a week, try to say something
kind to at least five people.

50

Lend a hand. If you see a
mother with a stroller who is
having trouble climbing stairs,
kindly offer to help.

"Never doubt that a small group of thoughtful, committed citizens can change the world; indeed, it's the only thing that ever has."

— MARGARET MEAD

51

Give warmth. Give blankets
you no longer use to a
homeless shelter. Go to
homelessshelterdirectory.org
to find locations in your area.

52

Support education. Buy from
fundraisers hosted by schools
in your neighborhood.

53

Remember a detail about a friend's life, and the next time you see them, ask about what they shared with you. Showing interest means a lot.

54

The saying goes, "Find a penny, pick it up and all day long you'll have good luck unless it's on tails." Create some luck! The next time you spot a penny on tails, flip it over to heads. Leave the penny there for someone to find and pass on the luck!

55

Volunteer at a local soup
kitchen for a day. Your efforts
will nourish more than just
empty stomachs.

56

Share your appreciation
of the arts. Bring a friend to
a favorite museum or attend
a play together.

57

Little things make a big
difference. Offer to help
a dressing room clerk by
putting some clothes away
on your way out.

"Kind words are the music of the world."

— F. W. FABER

58

Take the high road. If someone bumps into you, say "pardon me" instead of placing blame or getting angry.

59

Host a clothing drive in your neighborhood. It's a great way to get people together while also helping those in need.

60

Give a greeting! Every day
for one week, send a fun e-card
to different friends, family
members, or anyone dear to
you. Go to e-cards.com for tons
of free e-cards!

"Never part without loving words to think of during your absence. It may be that you will not meet again in this life."

— JEAN PAUL RICHTER

61

Share a positive attitude.
When someone says something
negative about another, say
something kind instead.

62

Give a pleasant surprise. Pay
for the meal of the person
behind you at the drive-thru.

63

Consideration goes a long way.
Let someone merge in front of
you in traffic.

64

Bring dinner to a family
with a new baby. They will
appreciate the extra help.

65

Be there for others. If you
encounter someone who is
feeling down, ask, "what can
I do to help?"

"Every man must decide whether he will walk in the light of creative altruism or in the darkness of destructive selfishness."

— MARTIN LUTHER KING JR.

66

Share little acts of kindness.
At work, take turns buying
coffee for each other with
co-workers.

67

Give kids the tools for success.
Purchase school supplies or
donate writing tools you don't
use to an underfunded school
in your area.

68

Share the joy of learning.
Visit firstbook.org to learn how
you can help give the gift of
reading to children from low-
income families.

69

Give to creatures great and small! Sign up to walk a dog at the local humane society. Visit hsus.org for more information.

Opportunities to give are
everywhere. After dining
out, package your leftovers
and offer them to a homeless
person on the way home.

71

Every day for a week, say something to make at least two people smile. A smile makes the world a brighter place.

5 GENEROUS ACTS
THAT TAKE NO MONEY

HUGS

KISSES

SMILES

WAVES

HANDSHAKES

72

Alleviate suffering. Order
flowers and have them delivered
to a local hospital addressed to,
"The Patient Most in Need of a
Brighter Day."

73

Join in the celebration of a
new life by sending a gift to a
family with a new baby.

74

Show appreciation. Send a note to a former teacher to share your accomplishments and say "thank you" for their influence on your life.

75

Giving is no accident. If you
spot a car with a flat tire, help
out the driver or call a tow
truck and wait with him or her
until help arrives.

"*It is always good to know, if only in passing, charming human beings. It refreshes one like flowers and woods and clear brooks.*"

— GEORGE ELIOT

76

The next time you have a bad
day, buy a plant or a bunch
of flowers for someone else.
Thinking about others changes
your perspective and will
make you feel good!

Inspire a younger generation
by organizing a car-wash
fundraiser with a local school.

78

Give a boost. In line at the
coffee shop, offer to buy the
person behind you a cup
of coffee.

*"Charity, good behavior,
amiable speech, unselfishness—
these by the chief sage have been
declared the elements of popularity."*

— BURMESE PROVERB

Give regularly. Choose a charity and set up an automatic payment through your bank to donate every month.

80

If someone in need asks
for a dollar, give without a
moment's thought. Lending
a hand will feel better than
keeping a dollar for yourself.

5 GENEROUS ACTS
FOR THE EARTH

RECYCLE. REUSE. REPAIR.

PLANT A TREE. GO TO
    EARTHSHARE.ORG FOR
    INFORMATION.

SAY "NO" TO BOTTLED WATER FOR
    A WEEK. MAYBE FOREVER.

SKIP THE DISPOSABLE CUP. FILL A
    TRAVEL MUG WHEN GETTING
    YOUR MORNING BREW.

DON'T WASTE WATER. TURN OFF
    THE FAUCET WHEN YOU WASH
    YOUR DISHES AND BRUSH
    YOUR TEETH.

81

Help make a change. Feed a
parking meter that has run out.

82

Give when you buy. Sign up at
igive.com to have a portion of
your on-line retail purchases
donated to charity.

"If you want others to be happy, practice compassion. If you want to be happy, practice compassion."

— DALAI LAMA

83

Reach across the world.
Donate to a child in need in
another country.

"A good deed is never lost: he who sows courtesy reaps friendship; and he who plants kindness gathers love."

— BASIL

84

Be generous to the Earth.
Plant a tree.

85

Spread some joy! Ask a local nursing home or hospital if you can help decorate rooms or communal areas for the holiday season, and gather friends and neighbors to join in.

86

Practice patience. If a car in
front of you is going slow, don't
honk.

*"Men do less than they ought,
unless they do all they can."*

— THOMAS CARLYLE

87

Give peace. Avoid fighting
for one week, no matter how
wronged you may feel.

88

Many hands make light work!
The next time you spot
someone who is moving, help
carry a few things, or offer
them a refreshing beverage.

89

Give fond memories. Create a
photo album of your favorite
memories for a friend or family
member.

90

Serve Thanksgiving Dinner to a neighbor who is alone. Generosity is the true spirit of the holidays.

91

Be sweet. Bake cookies or
cakes to raise money for a
school or a charity.

"*The habit of giving only
enhances the desire to give.*"

— WALT WHITMAN

92

Be supportive. Offer to drive a sick friend or neighbor to the doctor.

93

Cook a meal for a homebound friend. The gift of generosity will nurture long after the food is gone.

94

Take action and organize a
canned food drive in your office,
church, or community center.
Hopefully you'll inspire others
to reach out and help, too.

95

Spread the word. Host a theme party at your house to raise awareness and money for a good cause.

96

Show your support! Buy lemonade from a children's lemonade stand.

"Happiness does not consist in pastimes and amusements but in virtuous activities."

— ARISTOTLE

97

Get people talking . . . about
giving. Share your support of a
cause by wearing their t-shirt,
and share information about
the organization with others.

98

Bring beauty into the world.
Plant wildflowers in your yard
or at a local garden.

99

Give the gift of health and exercise. Donate an old bicycle that you no longer use.

*"Great effort from great motives
is the best definition of a happy
life."*

— WILLIAM ELLERY CHANNING

Organize a neighborhood garage sale. Encourage your neighbors to clear out their closets and donate any profits from the sale to a local organization. Giving back to your community will feel good—and it will be fun to make friends with your neighbors, too!

Love unconditionally and give generously.

"Love is, above all else, the gift
of oneself."

— JEAN ANOUILH (1910–1987)

You can show the world gratitude by simply learning to "Love unconditionally." If you can love at least one person unconditionally on a daily basis, then it would have a ripple effect on the rest of the world—and bring us closer to world peace and harmony.

There is no greater gift than simply being understood and accepted for being you. Celebrate the unique qualities of every person that makes up this beautiful world we live in. Take an interest in the cultural and religious differences of others. Travel to another country, read a book, or see a film about another point of view.

Love unconditionally, knowing that the person sitting next to you, living next to you, or living on the other side of the planet is human. Allow yourself to glow in love and generosity and you will see the reflection of light in everything around you.

With love,
Marnie & Tisha

WEBSITES OF INTEREST

bookcrossing.com

charity-charities.org

earth911.org/recycline

earthshare.org

e-cards.com

firstbook.org

goodsearch.com

homelessshelterdirectory.org

hsus.org

igive.com

mentor.com

redcross.org

uso.org

MY GOOD DEEDS

MY GOOD DEEDS